MEDITATIONS
FOR
COMPULSIVE PEOPLE

God in the Odd

Father Leo Booth

HEALTH COMMUNICATIONS, INC.
Pompano Beach, Florida

Father Leo Booth
St. Thomas of Canterbury Episcopal Church
Long Beach, California

Library of Congress Cataloging-in-Publication Data

Booth, Leo, 1946-
    Meditations for compulsive people.

    1.Meditations. I. Title.
BV4832.2.B629   1987   242   86-33640
ISBN 0-932194-44-3

Published by Health Communications, Inc.
Pompano Beach, Florida 33069

DEDICATION

This book is dedicated to

James E. Fulton, Jr.

A friend and collegue who enabled me to dream.

I wish to thank Barbara McRae for her many hours of patient typing and personal encouragement.

Also, Gloria Coker for her insightful sketches.

Preface

At different times in my life I have been accused of being a little "odd"; it is my hope that God can be found in the odd!

This series of meditations includes subjects that are not normally associated with God. It is my belief that God is to be found in His creation, in His creatures and in the every day imaginings and afflictions of His people.

A theme that runs through this book is compulsion, obsession; by this I mean behavior patterns and attitudes that cause pain: people can be addicted to people and "things" as well as chemicals!

The key to recovery is seeing,
                    accepting
                                 and talking about those things that stop us reaching our full spiritual potential. The miracle of creative living is discovered in the moves we make towards sanity, sobriety, serenity and acceptance.

I have placed at the end of each meditation a page for "study notes." Often when I am reading books that provoke in me feelings, I wished I could jot them down or record my reaction — it is my hope that the reader will record feelings and reactions that will lead to further growth, understanding and awareness.

"Meditations for Compulsive People: God in The Odd" is rediscovering divinity in the dust, in the ordinary things in life.

Fr. Leo

TABLE OF CONTENTS

CHARLIE CHAPLIN

"I remain one thing and one thing only and that is a clown.
It places me on a far higher plane than any politician."

Charlie Chaplin

"All I need to make a comedy is a park,

a policeman and a

pretty girl."

Charlie Chaplin

I liked him.

He was funny and sad.

Absurd, yet graceful.

A pertinent paradox.

A clown awkwardly dressed for dinner.

He revealed the world's comedy,

man's comedy,

my comedy.

In the laughter was the pain.

That really was his magic.

He spoke to me,

he made sense to me,

he reflected me — before I was born.

I felt I was his friend.

He needed me.

I wanted to protect him.

"Charlie." Oh yes, I knew him.

The cane.

The funny mustache.

The duck-like walk.

It was all an act to hide a fragile heart.

    Charlie, the gentle-man.

        The humorous protection plan.

            The clown who taught the world to laugh.

Oh yes, I knew Charlie.

    I knew his vulnerability.

    I knew his tears.

    I knew his fear.

    I knew his pain.

Forever misunderstood.

    Confused and confusing.

        Irritatingly lovable.

A drunk without a drink.

    An accident looking for a place to happen.

        A stumbling disease.

And yet, in a curious way, he healed me through my laughter.

    He showed me the stupidity of pomp and prejudice.

        He was a genius at revealing ordinary kindness.

A loving kiss to the lost child.

    .   A disheveled bouquet for his true love.

             A shared chicken dinner with a stray dog.

Nothing was an exact fit - that's the miracle.

        And that is where imitative man goes wrong - trying to be perfect!

Charlie's glance said he cared.

        His shrugging shoulders revealed persistence.

            His smile offered hope.

Oh yes, I knew Charlie.

GOD SAYS: A son of man in a badly fitting suit.

           An angel on the sidewalk.

           A miracle in the soup.

JESUS SAID: "We piped to you, and you did not dance;

       we wailed, and you did not mourn." (Matthew 11:17)

       I tried.

       I really tried.

In the clown is Truth reborn:

                 the blind see,

                  the lame walk,

and prejudiced men learn to bend.

In "Limelight" age seeks the solace of a young love,

and we all glimpse pathos in our lives.

A war is fought against "The Great Dictator" by the created art of mimicry.

Amid the laughter a blow is struck for freedom.

The miracle of God's Love carrying a cane;

that's Incarnation!

GOD SAYS: That is the tragedy of genius.

The little man battling the elements,

the reflector of every man's emotions,

the extraordinary power of the ordinary.

The tilting bowler hat on a curly head offers hope —

that's Spirituality!

Hope for the drug addict.

Hope for the gambler.

Hope for the lost child crying.

Hope for you and me.

Charlie allows the child in me to laugh,

play,

cry.

He stops the world from wallowing in its own seriousness.

He asks the businessman to find the banana skin.

Charlie is the risk.

GOD SAYS: The world has a happy ending,

       the homeless find rest,

           the widow will be comforted,

              the lonley love again;

                  I AM in the joke.

                  I AM the clown.

A THOUGHT: Why do I feel sad around Charlie?

       Why does he awaken in me pain?

       I cannot relax in his humor.

       He expects more from me;

       He expects more from the world.

NOTES

What feelings does this meditation arouse in me? _____

_____

_____

_____

_____

How can I use this meditation in my life? _____

_____

_____

_____

_____

2

THE
BOOGEYMAN

"A man should never be ashamed to say he has been
wrong, which is but saying, in other words, that
he is wiser today than he was yesterday."

Alexander Pope

"One who fears, limits his activities. Failure is only the
opportunity to more intelligently begin again."

Henry Ford

We all have known the boogeyman.

He hides in the shadows,

    the dark nights,

      the disturbing memories,

        yesterday's insanity.

We all have known, and know, the boogeyman.

He is the secret,

    the buried experience,

      the unsaid half-truth.

He is the symptom of Dis-ease.

      of Fear.

      of The Lie.

As a child I experienced him.

I was told he lived in the park,

    amongst the trees,

      down near the boats,

      clothed in darkness,

      blackness.

And I believed them.   I believed what I was told.

Often I walked near that park at night; I was always afraid.

Afraid he might grab me,

                 chase me,

                     eat me up.

I imagined his face,

                 brown and crinkled,

                     with green eyes and bad teeth.

He limped,

        wore a large black coat,

            and was silent.

I was twelve,

        I was afraid,

            and I believed in him.

               I believed in him.

Once I thought I saw him.

        He was running by the water near the boats.

            I ran away.

God, I still remember that fear.

That petrifying fear.

        My heart beat against my chest,

            my breath steamed,

               hot sweaty hands

and thumping headache.

Fear.

The more I believed the bigger he became;

the more I feared the more grotesque he became.

At fifteen I said I didn't believe in the boogeyman.

Yet I was still scared.

Scared of people.

Scared of places.

Scared of things.

Then I discovered alcohol.

For ten years the fears withdrew,

retreated for a time,

hid in the woods with the boogeyman.

Parties,

laughter,

sex,

power,

the world. Or so I thought!

Then the boogeyman came back.

I became afraid of the dark,

being alone,

going to work,

meeting people,

talking in public,

having sex,

being wrong,

being right.

I was afraid of my shadow; I was afraid of the boogeyman.

The more I drank the bigger he became;

the more I resisted the more grotesque he became.

Then an ordinary man, who said he understood, asked if I wanted to know where

the boogeyman lived?

"Where?" I asked.

"Inside you," he replied.

The boogeyman lived inside me.

The boogeyman was me.

The man understood.

The boogeyman is that secret,

that buried experience,

the other half of the half-truth.

The Lie.

I gave the boogeyman power;

    I made him big;

        I made him grotesque.

The boogeyman was the projection of my sickness,

                              fear,

                              guilt,

                              loneliness,

                              insanity.

                              My alcoholism.

In treatment I was told to confront the boogeyman.

I was told to run in the park,

    through the trees,

        down amongst the boats.

Grab the boogeyman,

    hold him,

        look at him,

            accept him.

                The boogeyman is me.

The boogeyman is the disease,

    and the disease is part of me.

My name is Leo, and I am an alcoholic!

In order to experience recovery I had to confront my disease;
    I couldn't go around it,
        below it,
           above it.
    I must go through it and hold it in my life.

GOD SAYS: The boogeyman is the fear that keeps you impotent,
        the fear that keeps you lonely,
           the fear that makes you a prisoner.

      Yesterday you believed The Lie; at times you still do.
      The Lie tells you: "You are no good."
          "You are ugly."
          "Have one drink."
          "You'll never lose that weight."
          "Vomiting keeps you thin."
          "Drugs make you happy."
          "Cocaine isn't addictive."
          "Everybody gambles."
          "Power and prosperity rest with others."

When you believe The Lie you give it power.

It has no power unless you believe it,

    encourage it,

        miss your "specialness."

Recovery means looking within —

    confronting the dark secrets,

        disturbing memories,

            yesterday's insanity.

Recovery means experiencing your given power,

    the love of self,

        the joy of your world.

A THOUGHT: God is saying to us: Welcome to my world,

        Won't you come on in,

        Miracles I guess

        Still happen now and then.

        Welcome to my world,

        And leave your cares behind,

        Welcome to my world

        Built with you in mind.

Knock, and the door will open,

Seek, and you will find,

Ask, and you will be given

The key to this world of mine.

Winkler &
Hathcock

And the key to this world is within you.

NOTES

What feelings does this meditation arouse in me? _____

_____

_____

_____

_____

How can I use this meditation in my life? _____

_____

_____

_____

_____

3

A Baked Bean

"This is the journal I kept every night at the Betty Ford Drug Center: 'Today is Friday. I've been here since Monday night. One of the strangest and most frightening nights of my life. Not to mention lonely. But I am not alone. There are people here just like me, who are suffering just like me, who hurt inside and out, just like me, people I've learned to love. It's an experience unlike any other I've known.' "

Elizabeth Taylor

"Only a fish can do an autobiography of a fish."

Carl Sandburg

What do you think about when the word "bean" is mentioned?

Food,

breakfast,

chili,

Mexico,

diarrhea.

What do you think about?

I think about loneliness,

isolation,

separation,

desperation.

As a child I dreamed that I was the last baked bean in the can,

sliding down the side,

slowly,

in a thick sauce,

ever so slowly

— and alone.

I cannot remember whether I shouted for help, but I know I was afraid.

Beans mean many things to many people, to me it means "lost-ness".

When I see them at the supermarket

or watch them advertised on the TV

or hear kids screaming for more beans,

a cold chill creeps down my spine

and I remember.

GOD SAYS: So you felt like a baked bean?

Now I've heard it all . . .

I made beans.

I can love you as a bean: but you are not a bean!

At some level, Leo, you knew and know that you are not a bean.

You only "felt" like a bean.

You felt insignificant,

you felt unimportant,

you felt "less than."

Isn't that addiction?

Many alcoholics know this feeling.

Many children of alcoholics know this feeling.

Many gamblers and their families know this feeling.

You felt like a piece of garbage.

I suppose a bean is the next best thing!

But you are not.

You never were.

You never will be.

And God said, "Let the earth bring forth living creatures according to their kinds: cattle and creeping things and beasts of the earth according to their kinds." And it was so. And God made the beasts of the earth according to their kinds and the cattle according to their kinds, and everything that creeps upon the ground according to its kind. And God saw that it was good.

Then God said, "Let us make man in our image, after our likeness; and let them have dominion over the fish of the sea, and over the birds of the air, and over the cattle, and over all the earth, and over every creeping thing that creeps upon the earth."

So God created man in his own image, in the image of God he created him; male and female he created them.

And God blessed them, and God said to them, "Be fruitful and multiply, and fill the earth and subdue it; and have dominance over the fish of the sea and over the birds of the air and over every living thing that moves upon the earth."

And God said, "Behold, I have given you every plant yielding seed which is upon the face of all the earth, and every tree with seed in its fruit: you shall have them for food. And to every beast of the earth, and to every bird of the air and to everything that has the breath of life, I have given every green plant for food." And it was so.

And God saw everything that he had made, and behold, it was very good. And there was evening and there was morning, a sixth day.

(Genesis 1:24-31)

GOD CONTINUES: Did you hear that? "And it was good."

I was saying that about you.

Know it.

You are good.

So many people hurt and rejected ME by discounting MY precious image that I placed within you.

In you I AM discovered.

I have given you everything.

You can think,

    read,

      write,

        play,

          cry,

            feel,

              love,

                dance,

                  make music,

                    have sex,

                      "walk on water ",

                        die with dignity.

My image is great,

        creative,

           yes, divine.

REFLECTION: But God, I did feel like a bean.

    I felt lost, lonely and isolated.

    I did!

GOD SAYS: I know.

    Because for a moment you forgot who you are.

    I AM in you,

      with you,

through you. Always.

Through you I make music.

make song,

make love,

— and, sadly at times, make war.

People are powerful, so powerful.

Yet still they do not use it,

hold it,

feel it.

Hence the baked bean.

That is the on-going blasphemy,

the disease of mankind,

the Grand Lie retold.

Man insults Me by insulting My image.

Pride in reverse — man rejects his greatness.

I offer the world — he sees a bean;

Adam, all over again.

The Fall, and no serpent!

A THOUGHT: Lord, now I see; help my blindness.

Now I feel Your Power; help my weakness.

Now I taste Your glory; help my darkness.

This bean is reaching for the stars.

NOTES

What feelings does this meditation arouse in me? _____

_____

_____

_____

_____

How can I use this meditation in my life? _____

_____

_____

_____

_____

4

OSCAR WILDE

"The universe is not to be narrowed down to the limits of understanding, which has been man's practice up to now, but the understanding must be stretched and enlarged to take in the image of the universe as it is discovered."

Francis Bacon

"Demanding and rejecting, criticizing and judging, 'righting' and 'wronging' are the sickness of the mind. To be free of distorted perceptions, see the chains of addictive patterns that dominate our consiousness and make our lives a battle.Our perception of others is only our projection of fears and desires for ourselves."

Kenneth Keyes

A witty man.

    A joker with a tear.

        A poet in outrageous lace.

You pushed us to understand.

    You ridiculed us into reality.

        You mesmerized us with the beauty of language
and still we crushed you.

We crushed your aspiring wisdom,

    we crushed the healing balm of your prose,

        we crushed your peculiar divinity.

We were afraid.

    Afraid to reconsider.

        Afraid to change.

            Afraid to trust something different.

And yet "the love that dared not speak its name" spoke —

    and today many are made whole.

You dented the armor of a prejudiced nation,

    you shamed the name of justice.

People are wiser for your life,

more cautious because of your imprisonment,

reflective on the nature of your love.

Oscar, you are a green carnation for tomorrow's people;

in you a kind of loving is made free.

GOD SAYS: A prophet's prophecy is rarely understood in his day,

a priest makes sacrifices with his life,

Oscar died and made men live with confusion.

Truth is rarely clear.

It often provokes fear and denial.

Truth is a double-edged sword.

When you pray to be true, beware.

When you ask for integrity, be prepared to pay.

Holiness hurts!

Oscar sought to make religion spiritual,

morality bearable.

The cost was self.

His love is rarely understood - even by the chosen.

It speaks beyond the physical,

it dreams beyond imaginings,

it rests in the bleeding heart of God.

Oscar battled hypocrites,
      fought "righteous" crusaders,
            challenged respectability.

Like all of us, he was his worst enemy.
He became addicted to his arrogance,
                  buffoonery,
                      intellectualism;
                          pride made war on his artistry.
His trial was a noble cause fought for a myriad of reasons —
      not all were pure.
           Such is the artist.

Somewhere in "Reading Gaol" his genius was purified.
      With his pain grew understanding.
           In his despair forgiveness was discovered.

Oscar unwillingly exchanged fame for sackcloth,
      and humbly reflected our beauty,
           our dreams and our aspirations.

Beauty in poetry,
      beauty in letters,

beauty in death,

    given in life;

He was MY artist.

A THOUGHT: Teach me to find Truth in the confusion of my life.

    In my failings and weaknesses, let me discover strength;

    through my addiction may I grow.

    Make my disease work for me.

NOTES

What feelings does this meditation arouse in me? _____

_____

_____

_____

_____

_____

How can I use this meditation in my life? _____

_____

_____

_____

_____

_____

_____

5

Wastepaper Bins

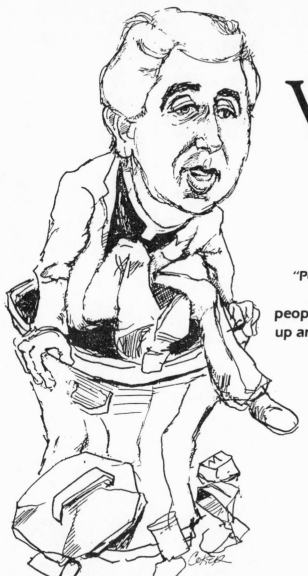

"People are always blaming circumstances for what they are. I don't believe in circumstances. The people who get on in this world are the people who get up and look for the circumstances they want, and if they can't find them, make them."

George Bernard Shaw

"We are what we think.

All that we are arises with our thoughts.

With our thoughts we make the world."

Buddha

For years I was a wastepaper bin.

I put garbage in my life — lies,

         negative thoughts,

         pornographic pictures,

         manipulation,

         pride,

         deceit,

         masks,

         "people-pleasing",

         arrogance,

         alcohol,

         ritual,

         plastic Madonnas,

         more alcohol,

         violence - verbal and physical.

Yes - a wastepaper bin is the victim of people's rubbish,

     and I was putting "crud" in my life!

Then it began to hurt,

     I began to feel the pain,

         I felt I was bursting.

I saw what I was becoming and I didn't like it.

     A wastepaper bin.

A SCENE: "Eugene, you are a clever young man.

  You have great talent,

                great potential,

                      a great future.

  You will be a success."

At twelve I heard that;

      At fourteen I repeated it . . . many times.

            "You will be a success."

Then silence fell.

What happened?

      Other things came into my life.

            Okay, I put other things in my life:

                  rock and roll,

                  girls,

                  girls and boys,

                  marijuana,

                  television,

                  alcohol,

                  noise,

                  deafening noise,

                  cocaine.

I'm sure I did some creative things, from sixteen to twenty — but I can't

  remember.

It was always — tomorrow I will do it.

Tomorrow I will go to school,

tomorrow I will stop,

tomorrow I will start,

tomorrow I will behave differently.

"Eugene, you are a clever young man.

You have great talent,

great potential,

a great future.

You will be a success."

But at what?

GOD SAYS: You can be a success because I created you.

You can have a great future because you are great.

I do not make junk.

But for years, Eugene, you threw away everything I gave you.

You stuffed yourself with trivia,

wastepaper,

"crud,"

drugs.

See what is happening.

See where you are going.

And then decide, really decide,

to be different.

That is recovery.

Two thousand years ago I met a rich young man who wanted to be different:

> As Jesus was starting on his way again, a young man ran up, knelt before him, and asked him, "Good Teacher, what must I do to receive eternal life?" "Why do you call me good?" Jesus asked him." No one is good except God alone. You know the commandments: 'Do not commit murder; do not commit adultery; do not steal; do not accuse anyone falsely; do not cheat; respect your father and your mother.' "
> "Teacher," the man said, "ever since I was young, I have obeyed all these commandments."
> Jesus looked straight at him with love and said, "You need only one thing. Go and sell all you have and give the money to the poor, and you will have riches in heaven; then come and follow me." When the man heard this, gloom spread over his face, and he went away sad, because he was very rich. Jesus looked around at his disciples and said to them, "How hard it will be for rich people to enter the Kingdom of God!"
>
> (Mark 10:17-23)

The rich young man wanted the trivia,

wastepaper,

"crud",

poison taken out of his life.

But he didn't want it enough!

Do you?

A THOUGHT: God, help me to love the world through being me.

Teach me to offer myself respect,

treat myself with dignity,

enjoy my integrity.

God, help me to love the world through loving me.

Notes

What feelings does this meditation arouse in me? _____

_____

_____

_____

_____

How can I use this meditation in my life? _____

_____

_____

_____

_____

_____

CAR KEYS

ALCOHOLISM

FREEDOM

COKER

"And only when we are no longer afraid do we begin to live in every experience, painful or joyous; to live in gratitude for every moment, to live abundantly."

Dorothy Thompson

"You can never get enough of what you don't need to make you happy."

Eric Hoffer

A SCENE: Court Room — "The court has decided to allow you to drive
again . . . Here are your car keys."

I remember this incident.
I remember the feelings of fear,

excitement,

joy,

shame.

Car keys.
They are part of my memory.

Part of my freedom.

Part of my sobriety.
For two years they were taken away from me.
I walked.
Rode a bicycle.
Pretended not to care.
Like a little boy, I was punished for driving under the influence of alcohol.

A necessary punishment.

A painful growth point.

Things can be taken away.

Nothing lasts forever if you abuse it.

"The court has decided to allow you to drive again . . . Here are your car keys."

I remember that day;
　　I cried,
　　　jumped for joy,
　　　　　hurt my foot,
　　　　　　　I cried with excitement.

Often I see the keys and secretly remember.
On a coffee table,
　　or beside a flower pot,
　　　　resting on my suede gloves,
　　　　　　— I remember.

I see the car crash,
　　hear the screams,
　　　　smell the dust,
　　　　　remember the "Moment."

I see powerlessness.
　　I see recklessness.
　　　　I see policemen.
　　　　　I feel pain.
　　　　　　I know unmanageability.
　　　　　　　Car keys: a remembered disease on a ring!

For two years I walked,

sulked,

　　　　rode a bicycle . . .

No car keys!

　　A symptom of alcoholism.

　　　　I remember.

JESUS SAID: "I will give you the keys of the kingdom of heaven." (Mk. 16:19)

But I wanted car keys!

For me to see the Kingdom the car keys had to be taken away;

　　　　having less brings more.

The keys are part of my sobriety,

　　　　　　my happiness,

　　　　　　　my joy,

　　　　　　　　my freedom.

My not being allowed to drive was part of my losing . . . and part of my winning.

　　A symptom of the dis-ease;

　　　　the keys of unmanageability.

"Cunning, baffling and powerful" — car keys.

Today I have them back — and more,

　　　　　　much more.

　　Today I have the keys for living,

　　　　　loving,

　　　　　　being,

and remembering.

In the remembrance is the hope for the future.

Today I am driving home,

    journeying into me,

        the mystery of being human.

The car keys take me into today.

        Who am I?

        What am I?

        Where am I going?

GOD SAYS: The keys of the Kingdom are to be found in the little things;

    a smile,

      a hug,

        choice,

          freedom.

A THOUGHT: Tucked away in our subconcious is an idyllic vision. We see ourselves on a long trip that spans the continent. We are traveling by train. Out of the windows we drink in the passing cars on nearby highways, of children waving at crossings, of cattle grazing on a distant hillside, of smoke pouring from a power plant, of row upon row of corn and wheat, of flatlands and valleys, of mountains and rolling hillsides, of city skylines and village halls. But uppermost in our minds is the final destination. On a certain day at a certain hour we will pull into the station. Bands will be playing and flags waving. Once we get there so many wonderful dreams will come true and the pieces of our lives will fit together like a completed jigsaw puzzle. How restlessly we

pace the aisles, damning the minutes for loitering — waiting, waiting, waiting for the station. "When we reach the station, that will be it!" we cry. "When I'm 18." "When I buy a new 450 SL Mercedes Benz!" "When I get a promotion." "When I reach the age of retirement, I shall live happily ever after!" Sooner or later we must realize there is no station, no one place to arrive at once and for all. The true joy of life is the trip. The station is only a dream. It constantly outdistances us. "Relish the moment" is a good motto, especially when coupled with Psalm 118:24:" This is the day which the Lord hath made; we will rejoice and be glad in it." It isn't the burdens of today that drive men mad. It is the regrets over yesterday and the fear of tomorrow. Regret and fear are twin thieves who rob us of today. So, stop pacing the aisles and counting the miles. Instead, climb more montains, eat more ice cream, go barefoot more often, swim more rivers, watch more sunsets, laugh more, cry less. Life must be lived as we go along. The station will come soon enough.

"THE STATION"
by Robert J. Hastings

NOTES

What feelings does this meditation arouse in me? _____

_____

_____

_____

_____

How can I use this meditation in my life? _____

_____

_____

_____

_____

7

SEX

"The teachers of the Law and the Pharisees brought in a woman who had been caught committing adultery, and they made her stand before them all. 'Teacher,' they said to Jesus, 'this woman was caught in the very act of committing adultery. In our Law Moses commanded that such a woman must be stoned to death. Now, what do you say?' They said this to trap Jesus, so that they could accuse him. But he bent over and wrote on the ground with his finger. As they stood there asking him questions, he straightened up and said to them, 'Whichever one of you has committed no sin may throw the first stone at her.' Then he bent over again and wrote on the ground. When they heard this, they all left, one by one, the older ones first. Jesus was left alone, with the woman still standing there. He straightened up and said to her, 'Where are they? Is there no one left to condemn you?' 'No one, sir,' she answered. 'Well, then,' Jesus said, 'I do not condemn you either. Go, but do not sin again.' "

St. John, Ch. 8

"Having put off her veils she stood before me; She
was beautiful and her body without defect. What
shoulders and arms I saw and touched! And the
shape of her breasts so suited to be caressed!
And under her breast, perfect and smooth was her belly,
And rich and large her thighs! Fresh with youth
her legs! Why tell all? I saw nothing that was not praise
worthy. And naked I clasped her to me. Who cannot
guess the rest? Both tired we rested."

"Amores"
Ovid

Sex; the gift of God that causes shame.

Why?

How silly!

But why?

God creates - and man (almost) immediately seeks to hide,

cover,

snicker,

and forever hurts himself on a fig leaf.

Like alcohol, sex can be used to avoid reality.

The sensual drug that is bottled within us.

Abuse it and we miss the gift

— and we all do, at times.

We need to look again,

        see,

        accept,

        surrender to the gift of sex . . . and live.

Sex is not ours — it is a gift.

Take the gift,

        hold the gift,

                caress the gift,

                        perspire in its heated beauty,

                              — and be grateful.

Sex is transformed into love by gratitude.

The lonely rub,

        the couple's ecstacy,

                the baby's cry for the future

        — they reflect the miracle of sex.

Make it more than it was meant to be and it becomes the abused abuser;

    make it less and you forever miss the gift.

        And you grow dry.

Accept it and it becomes part of the miracle of life.

    Isn't that what the Master meant when He said to the crowd,

        "He that is without sin among you, let him first cast a stone at her."

She (like the crowd) did not see the gift,

    she provoked in Jesus a tear rather than a stone.

      She was the victim.

We miss the gift when we make it an object,

    a crude magazine,

      an offensive joke,

        an end rather than a journey.

Who, at times, hasn't sold the gift?

    But still it remains.

    It remains within.

Sexuality is part of our patterned spirituality.

    The good and the bad,

      the active and the passive,

      the heat in the hand.

We are all angels in the dust.

A SCENE: I'm drinking coffee in a cafe.

    I feel bored,

      lonely,

        awkward.

    Then I see a young girl — alone.

    She looks cute.

      She is alone. I think, "I could use some of that tonight."

GOD SAYS: That is exactly the point, you would "use" her.

Just as you used pills,

cocaine,

booze,

— and now MY child.

I created her in love — to love,

to love and be loved,

to touch and be touched,

relationship.

Then you see her and want her,

want her to use her,

drink her,

fix her.

The same disease.

The same abuse.

The same unmanageability.

Sex, like freedom, can kill.

If compulsively sought it leads to slavery,

distruction,

and death.

So, tonight, you want to manipulate her,

take her,

use her,

— and tomorrow?

This kind of sex always brings pain,

probably pills,

cocaine,

alcohol.

And you are doing it.

See.

See.

In the using of the girl is the "slip,"

your slip,

addiction.

Respect her enough to let her go - and begin to love yourself.

A THOUGHT: Thank You for the joy of sex.

For the fun created by our bodies,

the ecstacy of the embrace,

God's natural high.

Teach us to be responsible in the pleasure,

respectful in the enthusiasm,

selfless in the need.

Sex is man's historical "yes" to life.

NOTES

What feelings does this meditation arouse in me? _____

_____

_____

_____

_____

How can I use this meditation in my life? _____ ____

_____

_____

_____

_____

8

A Nose With A Difference

"My old friend — look at me,
And tell me how much hope remains for me
With this protuberance! Oh I have no more
Illusions! Now and then — bah! I may grow
Tender, walking alone in the blue cool
Of evening, through some garden fresh with flowers
After the benediction of the rain;
My poor big devil of a nose inhales
April . . . and so I follow with my eyes
Where some boy, with a girl upon his arm,
Passes a patch of silver . . . and I feel
Somehow, I wish I had a woman, too,
Walking with little steps under the moon,
And holding my arm so, and smiling. Then
I dream — and I forget . . . And then I see
The shadow of my profile on the wall!"

"Cyrano de Bergerac"
by Edmond Rostand

"Rudolph, the red-nosed reindeer had a very shiny nose
And if you ever saw it, you would even say it glows.
All of the other reindeer used to laugh and call him names,
They'd never let poor Rudolph join in any reindeer games;
Then one foggy Christmas Eve, Santa came to say:
'Rudolph, with your nose so bright, won't you guide my sleigh tonight?'
Then how the reindeer loved him as they shouted out with glee:
'Rudolph, the red-nosed reindeer, you'll go down in history.'"

John Marks

Rudolph used his "difference";

        that is the key to living.

           Apparent ugliness becomes the vehicle for joy,

          usefulness,

            healing.

Santa Claus saw in Rudolph's nose his "specialness."

     The Gospel was rediscovered,

       the Talmud represented,

        the Koran rephrased.

       At-one-ment.

If only we could see beyond the shapes —

        into creativity;

        that is genius.

Those silly reindeer called him names:

yid,

nigger,

queer,

lush,

junkie.

Then something happens:

the deaf hear,

the blind see,

bigots forgive,

addicts recover,

families begin to talk,

fear takes a risk,

miracle.

GOD SAYS: I made you in difference,

I created you in variety,

I breathed into the patterned fabric of mankind.

And then you hid,

covered yourselves,

wore masks,

— and the pain grew.

For thousands of years man has been creating his pain —

and then complaining.

Even I was manipulated into the terror;

Jews killed Baalists,

Christians killed Jews,

Muslims killed Christians,

Protestants killed Catholics,

Catholics killed Protestants;

In MY name!

Prejudice used difference to destroy,

yet I created difference to enrich.

Rudolph heals "through a glass, darkly."

Cyrano offers Roxane the purest love: selflessness.

I REPLY: Yes Lord, the disease of dependency can be in religion.

It separates,

divides,

and isolates.

Each Sunday many gather for "a fix": exclusivism,

bigotry,

hypocrisy,

division.

"We are powerless over religion and our lives have become unmanageable."

A step in the right direction.

A THOUGHT: Lord, teach us how to hold hands with those we do not understand.

Let us risk in service,

grow in fellowship

discover the brightness of Your love in our difference.

NOTES

What feelings does this meditation arouse in me? _____

_____

_____

_____

_____

How can I use this meditation in my life? _____

_____

_____

_____

_____

9

DESIGNER JEANS

"Toast is my favorite food. I don't like to wear underwear with dresses in the summer because I like to enjoy the breezes. My first big moment was in high school when I was voted 'Class Individualist,' or actually acknowledged for being a freak. I just finished starring in an independent film which I've been doing for one-and-a-half years. When I'm not working I like to get wired and dance to reggae bands."

Julie Topetzes
(advertisment for designer
jeans, Seventeen Magazine,
February, 1985)

"For he, to whom the present is the only thing that is present, knows nothing of the age in which he lives."

Oscar Wilde

Designer jeans; such a sexy fig-leaf.

So little, and so stretched.

Graceful,

      seductive,

            comfortable,

                relaxing

                    and naughty.

Why?

      Because they put shape into sex.

                  You see it,

                      watch it,

                          think it;

                              imagination.

But more than just the obvious, designer jeans speak of:

      freedom,

            youth,

                abandonment,

                    gentle rebelliousness.

In this cloth is tomorrow woven.

      Youth united,

           dreams dreamed;

              a uniformed class-less-ness.

GOD SAYS: The body is beautiful:

legs,

thighs,

hips.

Enjoy yourself.

Enjoy others.

Be free.

In the designer jean is spontaneous freedom;

a blue revolution.

From county worker to city office boy;

superstar to computer supervisor;

relaxed royalty to desperate addict:

commonality walks in pants!

Here is visible music,

the faded dance,

the stretched poem,

art on a hip.

GOD SAYS: I AM in the fashion,

the crinkled line,

the stiffening zip.

Don't keep ME from your play — you modern troubadour;

don't keep ME out of the downtown ballet — in ordinary stores;

don't keep ME in the religious box;

let ME play in you!

REFLECTION: In the sculptured shapes He is perceived.

His beauty,

His flesh,

His creation.

And He is unisexed.

The girl in the man,

the man in the boy,

beauty in the beast,

divine sexuality.

GOD SAYS: But the joy,

excitement,

fun,

must be shared.

Those who have must freely give to those who have not.

The designer jean reflects a confidence in life that must be shared,

the music must be passed on,

the dance must be taught,

the world needs to be ONE.

We need each other.

THOUGHT: Thank You for clothes. For designers. For style.

Thank You for choice in fashion.

Thank You for my material blessings.

And in the "thank you" is the promise to share.

Those millions who need food,

those millions who need clothes,

those millions who need hope.

My gratitude must involve a promise to them

otherwise I am forever naked.

NOTES

What feelings does this meditation arouse in me? _____

_____

_____

_____

_____

How can I use this meditation in my life? _____

_____

_____

_____

_____

10

JOGGING

"Happiness is not in our circumstances but in ourselves. It is not something we see, like a rainbow, or feel, like the heat of a fire. Happiness is something we are."

John B. Sheerin

"I am an optimist. It does not seem much use to be anything else."

Winston Churchill

What has jogging to do with spirituality?

What has jogging to do with serenity?

What has jogging to do with sobriety?

Everything!

Jogging enables you to feel;

in the panting and the breathing is the living.

Man was not created to be cosmetic,

sterile,

plastic;

man was created from dust to sweat.

For "jogging" understand tennis,

walking,

aerobics,

gym work,

cycling,

bowling,

golf,

sex,

the physical.

Get physical and sweat;

feel your life in your body,

feel your body in your life.

God created man to create;

    the sculptured sculptures,

        the music plays,

            words make sound,

                a body feels.

Jogging — altered attitude.

    Now I am doing rather than talking,

        giving rather than taking,

            making rather than consuming,

                experiencing rather than spectating,

            living rather than existing.

            Jogging.

It is honest,

    real,

        healthy,

            good for me.

                Even the pain is good for me.

              The exertion is good for me.

            I smell human.

I begin to feel my energy,

    feel my body,

        feel my strength; divinity.

A rhythm comes into life.

Order.

Shape.

Movement.

I am going somewhere.

I am experiencing.

I am somebody.

"Hi" - a fellow jogger makes contact - then moves on.

Through this exercise I reach the elements.

Air touches my cheeks.

Sun and rain energize my journey.

Wind soothes me.

Glorious silence becomes mingled with the steps,

breath,

aches.

I experience the scenery of cars,

trees,

"stop" signs,

pedestrians,

bicycles;

it is all ONE.

To think that some yesterdays ago I was a drunk.

Couldn't run,

didn't smile,

wouldn't see;

sentenced to a bar.

Everything was pain:

pain in my head,

pain in my muscles,

pain in my relationships,

pain in my isolation.

ALCOHOLISM: Saying "no" to life.

Exchanging the stars for a gin.

Fantasy for reality.

A stagger for a jog.

GOD SAYS: I AM with you, son of man.

A THOUGHT: Jogging is part of my "yes".

My hope.

My creativity.

Spirituality is the continuing grasp for wellness: body,

                  mind,

                  emotions;

              — that is wholeness.

In the jog is the balance;

                endorphins released,

                  a natural high.

NOTES

What feelings does this meditation arouse in me? _____

_____

_____

_____

_____

How can I use this meditation in my life? _____

_____

_____

_____

_____

11

CAKE

"Sometimes I'd wake up in the morning and I would know that I was going to binge that day and I don't know why. Sometimes it was almost a reward. I'd think, 'I've been good, so I will reward myself.' It (binging) is the best feeling in the world. You don't have to worry about anyone around you."

Jill (Bulimic)

"Man is never attached to anything as his own suffering."

Gurdjieff

Cake — sweet poison!

For some it is a pleasant dessert — for others it is death.

"Have a little cake?" — and the agony begins.

"Only a little," I think to myself.

   "Okay, I'll just have one piece."

      I won't binge after that piece.

         Today will be different.

            Tomorrow I'll diet.

Now I've tasted it; I want more.

   God, I feel as if I'm bursting inside.

      I feel the blood rushing around my body.

         I still taste the cake.

            I need more.

               I want more.

                  More.

Always the same.

   Tomorrow I'll stop.

Each day I die a little inside.

   I want to be thin,

      and yet I'm scared to be thin.

I'm in no-man's land!

I'm afraid to be beautiful

> and I hate, really hate, being fat.

I hate my body — I avoid looking at my body.

> Cover it up,
>> cover the flab;
>>> avoid mirrors,
>>>> avoid me.

God, nobody could like me.

> No boy has ever asked me out.
>> Girlfriends are now asking me to babysit on Fridays!

I'm so lonely,

> so scared,
>> so fat.
>>> Fat, fat, fat . . . I hate my fat!

Some years ago I thought I'd found a solution:

>> Vomiting.

When I heard about it in the newspapers I thought it was awful,

>>> gross,
>>>> kinky.

But the idea stayed with me.

One day after a two-day binge I tried it.

It worked.

I felt empty.

Felt good.

And the pain seemed to satisfy.

A good pain.

The pain,

punishment,

hurt,

felt right.

The hurt felt good;

the pain felt good;

the punishment felt good.

Addiction.

Dependency.

Obsession and compulsion.

I deserve to hurt. That was God punishing me!

With the vomiting followed the laxatives,

diuretics,

and regular binge/vomiting.

Sometimes six times a day.

Like the alcoholic I carried gum,

      looked for restrooms,

           washed my mouth out,

         and felt ashamed!

             Always the shame.

               Always the guilt.

I lost twenty pounds in 1981.
In 1982 I gained fifty.

Nobody knew.

    Can you believe that?

        Nobody knew my pain.

          Felt my loneliness.

            Heard my tears.

"A little more cake, Alice?"
"Okay," I said.

GOD SAYS: Alice, I see your tears,

        feel your pain,

           know your loneliness.

   People can be crucified with cake.

   The disease lives in the secret.

People do not hear,

        understand,

                support — because they do not know.

People live and die in the secret.

You are killing yourself: suicide.

    In the secret the disease is fed.

        In the fear the disease grows.

        In the isolation death creeps in.

Alice, "shout" for what you need. Make the people hear.

    Bartimaeus shouted two thousand years ago and I heard him.

    Lepers walked,

        the deaf touched ME,

        sinners knelt;

        you must "do" something.

Never tell Me you can't — tell Me you won't;

    never tell Me you are helpless — tell Me you are proud.

    Never tell Me nobody cares — I AM and I DO!

A THOUGHT: Lord, help people to confront. Confront pain to loose pain. Help those with eating disorders discover the strength that comes from sharing their pain. Help those muted by fear to find the courage to "shout."

Alice, there are thousands out here to help but we need to know where you are. Make contact; let us love you until you begin to love yourself.

82

NOTES

How does this meditation make me feel today? _____

_____

_____

_____

_____

How can I use this meditation in my life? _____

_____

_____

_____

_____

12

COMPUTERS

"Something begins me and it had no beginning;
something will end me, and it has no end."

Carl Sandburg

"The fool who knows he is a fool is that much wiser. The
fool who trusts he is wise is a fool indeed."

Buddha

Man's modern magic box.

        A click,

                buzz —

                        and an answer.

A brain at a switch,

               instant solutions,

                        a thousand alternatives made visible in seconds.

                        Miracle with a plug.

Is man coming of age?

           Is man reaching beyond his age?

                  Is tomorrow made possible now?

GOD SAYS: Man is still struggling for the fruit in the Garden.

           Computers are creative.

           My Genesis theme continues today,

                        " . . . and it was good."

           Computers are good.

They assist aviation,

            space research,

            hospitals,

             police,

              schools,

               news,

grocery lists,

ecological engineering,

recreation,

games,

the deaf and disabled.

The computer is modern man's wheel!

It is man's manufactured help-mate.

It assists,

directs,

and stimulates our tomorrows.

But it can never replace the genius of man

As man is dependent on ME,

so is the software dependent on man.

Those inner wires,

small bright lights,

sporadic whistles and beeps — You made them.

The answer is in the man.

They all need to be serviced,

cared for,

read,

switched on.

The computer is dependent.

It needs to be fed,

connected,

programmed.

It records and builds upon that which has first been given.

Computers are receivers.

Electrical butlers!

The productivity is incredible,

instantaneous,

and unforgettable —

but secondary.

The answer is always in the man.

GOD CONTINUES: "I created man in my own image."

I live in life — not 'things.'

The danger lies in man's ability to create idols.

The idols have included: the moon,

wind,

lightning,

totem poles,

witch doctors,

popes,

preachers,

dogma,

alcohol,

people,

sex,

and yes, computers.

To seek the comfort outside is addiction.

Man climbs from MY garden of freedom into the box.

He seeks to escape responsibility in 'things.'

Frankenstein is always the man

but the monster comes from within.

In man's image is choice found,

the mystery of being human.

the miracles of being free.

But with that freedom comes . . .

Addiction.

REFLECTION: Why do we seek God in things?
Idols,

witch doctors,

alcohol,

cocaine,

people,

computers. Why?

Because man seeks to understand,

        control

          and play God.

      Only in the mystical confusion of freedom is God to be found.

Man was created to make miracles:

      in man is the Love that creates,

          energizes,

            fashions,

              stimulates,

                and heals.

To seek the solution "in the box" is The Lie.

An unrealistic expectation of the computer is an abuse of the computer —

      an abuse of man.

Dependency places the power in the inanimate;

      an idol in the fruit!

I am learning to love me in my use of the world,

      in my use of what man has created,

        in my awareness of God in me,

I see potential disease with the computer,

      man is becoming lazy,

fat,

dehumanized,

institutionalized,

computerized.

"My kingdom for an Apple."
Man becomes the slave of his own creation;

lost in the flash,

light,

whistle,

buzz.

Man forgets to feel,

forgets to dream,

forgets to be wrong,

forgets his Garden.

God's life is in the bleeding,

kissing,

touching,

loving,

risking,

forgiving,

— and being confused again!

A THOUGHT: God, help us never to hide in our knowledge,

in our solutions,

in our clean answers,

in our precision.

Let us not be antiseptic;

let us play in the dust,

the dirt You made us from,

as angels in the dirt!

NOTES

What feelings does this meditation arouse in me? _____

_____

_____

_____

_____

How can I use this meditation in my life? _____

_____

_____

_____

_____

_____

13

DANCE

"See the music,
    hear the dance."
        George Balanchine

"Imagination is more important than knowledge."
        Albert Einstein

In dance we see God playing,

    music takes on form,

        the majesty of humanity.

Dance is the basic rhythm in life that is forever optimistic;

    it is clean,

        pure,

          and real.

Life is reflected in dance;

    the drama,

        the hope,

          the celebration.

In the dance man's pathos is perceived.

In the folk dance is the roots of our yesterdays.

    The history of a people,

        the style of a custom,

          the movement of tradition.

People clown,

    clap hands,

        form lines

          and make a circle.

Folk dance emphasizes our variety,

        our difference,

             our quaintness — and it is fun.

In the ballroom dance we demonstrate our formality,

          gesture

            and elegance.

Dress,

    musical precision

       and rehearsed discipline flow with reserved excitement.

The tango,

    fox trot

       and waltz bring a feeling of God's order to movement.

Ballet brings together drama and fantasy, mingled with romance.

    In the movement is the music,

       each step articulates a note,

         the characters are God's instruments.

Love is expressed without words.

    Feelings are made real in shapes and energy.

      Hope and tragedy abound.

Dance takes mankind beyond speech;

    beyond the word, into God.

Pop, punk and modern dance make the spectator feel alive.

The participants know that there is more,

more in life,

more to come,

more.

We miss God in so much of his handiwork.

In the movement of dance Truth is struggling to be seen.

In the choreographed story something of God is being revealed.

In Dance we catch God playing!

REFLECTION: Dance.

Movement that has been blessed.

An escape that returns home.

It brings the physical into the imaginative,

take form into IDEA,

makes reality dress in fantasy.

GOD SAYS: I AM the dance and I still go on.

In the jump,

leap

and deliberate twirl,

I AM alive.

You think too small.

     My prophesy is in movement.

       My forgiveness has a shape.

        I heal in the dance.

THOUGHT: Lord, help us to see Your beauty in physical words;

    In the punk rocker,

        jazzed roller

              and downtown breaker.

   Man has a thousand ways of saying "yes",

     creation is speaking,

       let us say it in dance,

         the dance of life.

NOTES

What feelings does this meditation arouse in me? _____

_____

_____

_____

_____

How can I use this meditation in my life? _____

_____

_____

_____

_____

14

A Tear

"Sometimes by taking the ordinary and isolating it, twisting it in a different direction or light, looking at it from a different perspective or in a different material, we see something that was always there, but we 'know' it for the first time."

Donald Pollard

"Truth - the beginning.
Peace - the meaning.
Love - the essence."

Kriensky

So much in so little: a tear.

So much love,

grief,

pain.

The feeling of love is so excruciatingly exhilarating.

We ache with happiness.

Shake with a cluster of feelings.

Are ecstatic with a joy that radiates from another human being.

We are in love — and we shed tears.

A spiritual experience is epitomized in that drop of water

trickling down a soft cheek.

Love is many but always one.

A mother observes her son growing into a man,

a daughter meets a man and feels a woman,

in the softness of a gentle night a marriage is made physical,

a dreamer's dream is achieved after forty years, —

in all these "moments" a tear of joy is shed.

And sometimes, in the silence of a solitary life, we shed a tear in a profound love of Self.

The ultimate is reached,

the physician begins to heal himself,

we begin to love ourselves.

A tear is shed in grief,

    a sense of loss,

        impotency,

            and helplessness.

A thousand griefs are experienced each day;

    a marriage is over,

        a child is dead,

            yesterday's youth is gone.

Buried feelings of yesterday's pain are resurrected by a remembrance;

    photograph,

        voice,

            an inscribed "I love you" in an old book,

              another person's sharing —

              and we remember.

With the sense of loss comes the grief,

              the helplessness,

                the tear.

Why did she die?

    If I only knew then what I know now!

        Why did it take so long for me to get sober?

Grief is experienced and a tear is shed.

And often with the tear is pain.

The pain of man's violence to man,

                    apartheid,

                  prejudice,

                judgment,

              ridicule,

                exploitation,

              famine,

              and addiction,

The tear reminds us that the pain is ours,

      its roots is in our reality,

         in our flesh,

           we bleed.

Relief comes with the sharing of painful feelings: guilt,

                              rejection,

                          fear,

                            anger,

                              rage,

                                isolation.

Without the tear we would burn alive, inside.

We realize our powerlessness,

    that we are not perfect,

        the dance of life goes on,

            we wipe the tear and await the next.

GOD SAYS: The tear is the fruit of living.

        As the plants need water to grow,

            so you need to cry in order to live,

                      create,

                    heal,

                     reconcile,

                      forgive.

                       feel.

I SAY: Lord, in the tear is the hope?

GOD REPLIES: Yes

A THOUGHT: God spare me from apathy!

      So long as I feel, I live.

      So long as I am able to love,

            experience grief,

           realize joy,

            shed a tear . . . I live.

NOTES

What feelings does this meditation arouse in me? _____

_____

_____

_____

_____

_____

How can I use this meditation in my life? _____

_____

_____

_____

_____

15

Hugs

"If you ever find happiness by hunting for it,
you will find it as the old woman did her lost spectacles
— on her nose all the time."

Josh Billings

"Happiness? It is an illusion to think that more comfort
means more happiness. Happiness comes of
the capacity to feel deeply, to enjoy simply, to think
freely, to risk life, to be needed."

Storm Jameson

Hugs: Demonstrable humility.

> They say I need you.
>
> > Need your touch,
> >
> > > need your warmth,
> > >
> > > > need your strength.
> > > >
> > > > > They say I need you.

Human problems require human solutions:

> "Don't tell me — show me."
>
> "Don't just tell me you love me — show me."

A SCENE: A support group had been organized for people who were lonely; those who had nowhere to go in the evenings. People met together to talk over coffee and cookies. Widows, bachelors, divorcees and people who were feeling alone with their problems met together to talk and exchange ideas.

Then one evening a stranger walked into the back of the room. He was covered in black leather and chains. He took some coffee, left the cookies, and sat at the back. He had a mustache and beard, boots and a leather hat: the uniform of machismo. He winced, scowled and occassionally grunted. Everybody looked; his presence was alarming. The woman who had been sharing became nervous and eventually fell into silence. For a minute nothing was said; it seemed like an eternity.

"Oh dear," I thought. Immediately I wanted to fix the problem with a statement — that's priest-craft!

Then an old Jewish lady got up from her chair, placed her coffee on a side table and walked over to the man.

She looked at him,

        smiled,

               and hugged him.

She held him,

        touched him,

               felt his pain.

Unlike the rest of us,

        she did not stare

           or look away,

               or nervously drink coffee;

               she held him,

                  she felt his pain.

Within moments he had placed his arms around the woman and was holding her.

He buried his head into her loving shoulders and audibly wept.

He poured his pain into her.

        He cried like a baby.

        She held him like a mother.

For several minutes this encounter took place.

Many in the room silently cried.

Some held hands.

Others prayed for such courage;

        the courage of the woman,

           the courage of the man.

After he had received his communion he gently pulled away and she returned to her seat,
        picked up the coffee,
                and sat down.

Then he began to talk.
        His name was Henry.
        He was a recovering alcoholic and heroin addict.

He was lonely,
        frightened,
                fearful
                        and afraid.

He needed to be held,
                touched
                        and hugged.
He did not need a statement!

The uniform was a mask.
        It covered the pain,
                loneliness
                        and fear.

        With the hug came the miracle.

The old woman took a risk,

she loved unconditionally,

she risked rejection,

such is Spirituality.

GOD SAYS: Do you remember these words?

"Woe to you, scribes and Pharisees, hypocrites!
For you are like whitewashed tombs, which
outwardly appear beautiful, but within they
are full of dead men's bones and all uncleanness.
So you also outwardly appear righteous to men,
but within you are full of hypocrisy and iniquity."

(Matthew 23:27)

Things are not what they seem.

Behind the white marble stone was rotting flesh.

Behind the uniform was the hurting child.

Things are not what they seem;

anger is fear dressed up.

REFLECTION: In the hug is the healing.

And the hug can be in a word,

touch,

or smile.

A hug is our insides reaching out to others,

ourselves,

the world.

God is to be found in a prophet,

a poet,

a song

and a hug.

A THOUGHT: God, when I reach out to my enemies I begin to understand something of myself. In arrogance I hear my own insecurity. When I befriend the lonely I discover my untouched strength. God, in Your variety I discover me.

NOTES

What feelings does this meditation arouse in me? _____

_____

_____

_____

_____

How can I use this meditation in my life? _____

_____

_____

_____

_____

16

THE EMPEROR'S NEW CLOTHES

"And so the Emperor set off in the procession under the beautiful canopy, and everybody in the streets and at the windows said, 'Oh! how superb the Emperor's new clothes are! What a gorgeous train! What a perfect fit!' No one would acknowledge that he didn't see anything, so proving that he was not fit for his post, or that he was very stupid. None of the Emperor's clothes had ever met with such success. 'But he hasn't got any clothes on!' gasped out a little child. 'Good heavens! Hark at the little innocent!' said the father, and people whispered to one another what the child had said. 'But he hasn't got any clothes on! There's a little child saying he hasn't got any clothes on!'
'But he hasn't got any clothes on!' shouted the whole town at last. The Emperor had a creepy feeling down his spine, because it began to dawn upon him that the people were right. 'All the same,' he thought to himself,

'I've got to go through with it as long as the procession lasts.' So he drew himself up and held his head higher than before, and the courtiers held on to the train that wasn't there at all."

Hans Christian Andersen

"Life is not having and getting, but about being and becoming."

Matthew Arnold

GOD SAID: Let there be light.

MAN SAID: No! Let us see things that are not there;

see things that others say they see,

let us not be awkward,

different,

or real.

Let us not "rock the boat."

The Emperor's new clothes.

"But he hasn't got any clothes on!" gasped the little child.

The game ends.

Shame on the child!

No. Shame on the game.

Truth is about being real: the uncovered,

the revealed,

light.

The Lie imitates a quest for knowledge.

The Lie pretends to seek for Truth.

The Lie says, "have more,"

but means, "get less."

"The Emperor's New Clothes" — or —

"Things Are Not What They Seem."

A SCENE: How are you feeling?

"Fine," says Ann.

Yet she had been eating all night,

eating and binging,

frightened,

angry,

lonely,

tired.

"Fine," said Ann.

"Will you babysit for us tonight?"

"Sure," says Ann.

But inwardly the voice cries out, "When will I have some fun?"

"I hate to say 'no'."

"I can't tell anyone what I feel."

"I hate living this way."

"I hate eating and binging,

being angry and smiling,

being empty and smiling,

dying inside and binging."

"Sure," says Ann.

Things are not what they seem;

the Emperor's new clothes.

Then a young boy cries, "The Emperor has no clothes on."

Ann asks for help;

she talks about her eating,

loneliness,

anger,

rage.

Ann talks about her feelings.

GOD SAYS: Let there be light.

Do not cover what needs to be seen.

Do not hide what should be known.

Speak and the fear fades.

"Abandon youself to God as you understand God. Admit your faults to Him and your fellows.

"Clear away the wreckage of your past. Give freely of what you find and join us.
We shall be with you in the Fellowship of the Spirit, and you will surely meet some of us as you
trudge the road of Happy Destiny."

(Alcoholics Anonymous)

That creative child in me hates The Lie,

longs to grow,

hungers for what is real.

I know when I have no clothes on,

I know when I pretend,

I know my masks;

Lord, let me accept this — and move to the Truth.

A THOUGHT: Lord, I want to live and be honest,

feel and speak out,

touch and be known,

live through my nakedness.

To hide behind food,

drugs,

relationships,

money,

religion — is to die.

Today I will not suffer in the smile;

suffocate in the shame;

die in the "feel fine."

NOTES

What feelings does this meditation arouse in me? _____

_____

_____

_____

_____

How can I use this meditation in my life? _____

_____

_____

_____

_____

17

THE CASINO

"The price of greatness is responsibility."

Winston Churchill

"Wealth consists not in having great possessions,
but in having few wants."

Epicurus

I remember this place. The M.G.M., Las Vegas.
The lights,
    girls,
        free drinks,
            flashing slot machines;
                I remember this place.

Ten years ago I nearly died here.
    Dean Martin sang songs,
        people applauded,
            and I nearly died here.

I was a gambler.
I didn't just gamble; I was a gambler.
    Some people drink — others are alcoholics.
    Some people eat — others are bulimics.
    Some people smoke "grass" — others are drug addicts.
        I was a gambler.

In a weekend I could lose everything.
    Lose my salary.
        the savings,
            the borrowed money,
                casino credit;

I could loose everything!

Eventually I did loose everything: my family,

my wife,

my children,

my job,

my self-respect.

Almost my life.

I cheated to gamble,

stole money to gamble,

prostituted myself to gamble.

Nothing compared with the chance of winning.

I remember it started so innocently.

I won a trip to Las Vegas.

I didn't want to go — my wife insisted;

funny now to remember — my wife insisted I go to Las Vegas!

"Let's have some fun and feed the slot-machines," she said.

"Something might happen."

It did.

We won five thousand dollars in thirty minutes.

The next morning, early, at 5:00 am, I went into the casino again.

Alone.

It looked just the same.

Lights,

    people,

        flashing slot-machines,

            smell of cigarettes and booze.

It felt warm; inviting.

    I played roulette. I won.

        Never had I ever felt like I felt.

        It wasn't the winning, it was the playing.

The chips on the smooth green table,

    the spectators watching me,

        the expressionless faces of the players — especially the winners!

I felt at home — winning or losing.

That is how it began.

    For the next two years I won some and lost many -

        but it didn't matter.

    I was playing,

        I felt good.

        The casino made me "high."

Soon I escaped from work to Las Vegas,

    disappeared from home on weekends to Las Vegas,

        preferred Las Vegas to family,

  wife

                                        sex,

                                        food,

                                        drink,

                                        anything!

I knew I was hooked.

          For eight years I knew I was hooked.

                    I lost almost everything knowing I was hooked.

                    I became a gambler without a hand!

I didn't think that anybody would understand.

I had never heard about my problem on television,

                                        documentaries,

                                        magazines

                                                  or in newspapers.

Then a close friend sent me an article on compulsive gambling.

The article described me.

          Women,

                    widows,

                              movie stars,

                                        journalists,

                                                  all behaved like me.

I took a throw on Gamblers Anonymous.

I walked into the smoke filled room,

saw the table and the speaker,

heard the sharing,

drank my coffee

and knew I was in the right place.

As in the casino, but differently, I knew I was at home.

The night of sharing,

the camaraderie,

the perceptive awareness enabled me to stay,

or at least come back.

That was six years ago.

Now I stand outside the casino that nearly killed me —

on my way to a meeting!

Today I want to stay outside the casino more than I want to go in.

That is a miracle.

A day at a time I choose life,

I choose living,

I choose my right to choose.

Inside the casino I have no choice.

I'm not perfect.

Today I have found a God that I can understand.

A spirituality that includes people.

A love of self.

Oh yes — next weekend I'm having dinner with my wife and children.

       Miracle in the ordinary.

GOD SAYS: I AM to be found in the choice.

       The casino was born in the Garden of Eden.

         People are still gambling on fruit,

           and people are still losing.

       Freedom is the ultimate gamble.

         I was prepared to make a choice for freedom.

           Prophets and sages, discussing a thousand different

              problems and situations, still bring the ultimate gamble

              into today.

       In our choice is the prize to be discovered.

A THOUGHT: Let me pray every choice

         and live every action.

       May I never put myself in dangerous places,

             dangerous situations;

                taking unnecessary risks.

       May I accept my imperfection with responsibility.

NOTES

What feelings does this meditation arouse in me? _____

_____

_____

_____

_____

How can I use this meditation in my life? _____

_____

_____

_____

_____

18

THE NAZIS

"If someday we are compelled to leave the scene of history we will slam the door so hard that the universe will shake and mankind will stand back in stupefaction."
Joseph Goebbels

"It is too late to save yesterday's victims . . . But it is not too late to save ourselves. The next time we truly hear the word Holocaust, it will be preceded by the word atomic. We had better learn from whom we can, while we can. Even from the Angel of Death himself."
Elie Wiesel

Boots.

   Regardless of where, when or how — always the boots.

     In the boots was the corrupt power,

       functional sexuality,

         cowardly violence,

           screaming demagogues,

             The Lie.

For a time the world went mad in a particular race,

   at a particular time,

     for a particular reason:

       Power.

   And that "particular" reflects you and me.

Power, the ultimate drug,

   man's natural opium,

     the "high" in the Fall.

God said to Adam: "This fruit you cannot have."

       Why? said the serpent to the woman.

       Why? said the woman to the man.

       Why? said Adam to himself.

    Eventually God was to ask them all, "Why?"

     Adam blamed the woman;

     Eve blamed the serpent;

The serpent blamed . . .

The "cappos" blamed the guards,

the guards blamed the S.S.,

the S.S. blamed the politicians,

the politicians blamed Hitler,

and Hitler blamed the Jews . . .

The Jews asked the world, "Why?"

Boots.

The answer is in the boots;

the answer is in man,

— in you and me.

When I drank I destroyed,

hurt,

fought,

behaved arrogantly,

dreamed murder,

screamed insults,

played God in black boots.

The drug was alcohol,

or cocaine,

or power,

or sex,

or racial superiority — all the same.

All an escape.

All a lie.

I blamed my family,

my job,

the church,

too many problems,

. . . God.

A lie.

Adam blamed the woman.

Eve blamed the serpent.

The serpent blamed . . .

and so it goes on.

A lie.

GOD SAYS: I AM against "sin" because it does not work.

Sin divides,

separates,

destroys,

and always lies.

Sin plays the serpent against the woman,

the woman against the man,

and man against himself.

Sin plays race against race,

       church against state,

              a son against his family.

                    Auschwitz.

Rather than resting in what is given, man takes what is not his.

       Fruit from the forbidden tree,

              pleasure in drugs,

                    power at the expense of people.

People see — but look in another direction.

People cry — but forget the pain.

People beg forgiveness — but continue the memory of the boots.

Oh yes, sin can wear boots!

Man wore a uniform,

       pretended to be what he was not,

              hid in appearances,

                    exchanged reality for fantasy,

                         forgot it was his flesh he was burning,

                           his bones he was crushing,

                             his hair he was collecting.

                    Man makes his judgment.

Power:

  alcohol,

    gambling,

      racial hatred,

        boots — all false dependency.

GOD CONTINUES: I AM against sin because it does not work.

      I gave you it all,

        you carry MY image.

      Spirituality is about building bridges,

        forgiving past injustices,

          risking in fear.

 Each time I stay silent,

      tell a lie,

        manipulate . . . I put on boots.

A THOUGHT: I heal when I discover the Nazi in me.

      Those times I dismiss without listening,

      hate without understanding,

      condemn because I am afraid.

NOTES

What feelings does this meditation arouse in me? _____

_____

_____

_____

_____

_____

How can I use this meditation in my life? _____

_____

_____

_____

_____

_____

19

MY NAME IS SHAME

"Humanity takes itself too seriously. It is the world's original sin. If the caveman had known how to laugh, history would have been different."

Oscar Wilde

"No one can develop freely in this world and find a full life without feeling understood by at least one person . . ."

Dr. Paul Tournier

I came upon you — when you were young.

When you were very young:

   before you understood,

      before you could speak,

         before you realized I was there.

I came upon you.

I created feelings of unworthiness,

      disgust,

         inferiority,

            ugliness,

               ·stupidity,

                  poverty

                     and difference.

         I tarnished the image of God.

I existed before the guilt.

   I live before the action.

      I was the whisper before the sound.

Always, I enter through the backdoor,

      unseen,

         unwanted,

            the first to arrive.

Guilt grows in me.

       Guilt finds its strength alongside me.

         I mold guilt into shape:

            My name is Shame.

The World asks, "Where does Shame come from?"

         From anywhere and everywhere.

The condescending glance from a parent.

       The awkward appearance in the mirror.

        The cruel remark from children.

           Feelings and actions condemned by the preacher.

          The touch that does not feel right.

I come from anywhere and everywhere!

I can transform the black,

        jew,

          gay,

            woman into nigger,

                 yid,

                  queer,

                 bitch.

I bring the pain that does not go away.

Shame. My name is Shame. And I live in negativity.

I make you feel dirty,

guilty,

"less than",

inferior.

My tools are prejudice,

fear,

control,

anger,

and imperfection.

I take what you are,

what you have,

how you look — and abuse you with it.

And you allow it!

From the hispanic to the sensitive cripple,

I make you feel less,

different,

helpless,

and alone.

GOD ASKS: Why do they give you such power? How can they miss the beauty that is within?
When will it stop?

REFLECTION: Because of Shame, people see only ugliness,

fat,

smallness,

disfigurement,

failure,

sin,

uncleanness.

They have become prisoners of self.

Chained by self-pity and remorse.

They miss the miracle and hold the pain.

That touch!

The neighbor's indiscreet touch,

the hand that rubbed,

pressed,

penetrated,

hurt

and abused.

Shame created guilt — even in the child!

And yet you were never to blame.

    You did nothing.

        You did not understand

                and still you blamed yourself.

The voice of Shame condemns — again and again.

    "You allowed it."

        "You never said anything."

            "You knew he would come back."

People are cruel to themselves.

    They abuse themselves.

        They bring the pain into their lives.

How?

By attacking their true selves.

    "I look so ugly. Everybody is looking at my spots."

        "I am too small. Too thin. Too hairy."

            "Why was I born Jewish? I hate my culture. I despise my parents."

        "I don't want to be gay. I must hide my gayness.

          I must never let anyone know my secret."

Often parents feed Shame with thoughtless remarks:

"You will never amount to anything. You are stupid."

"Why can't you be like your sister?"

"Are you a boy or a girl? Why aren't you playing sports?"

"It was a mistake to have you. I should have had an abortion."

"If you loved me you would not behave like this!"

"People who do these things are going to Hell."

"Children should be seen and not heard."

"God punishes disobedient children."

GOD SAYS: But I created you to be free.

You are not perfect but you are special.

I love you . . . and I want you to love yourself.

I respect you . . . and I want you to respect yourself.

You have dignity . . . reach for the stars.

SHAME SAYS: "I came upon you — when you were young.

When you were very young:

before you understood,

before you could speak,

before you realized I was there.

I came upon you."

I REPLY: But I do not have to listen.

Today I am beginning to see my beauty.

I rejoice in my difference.

I am discovering my power,

I do not have to live in yesterday.

I can change.

I can dream.

I can create a positive life,

a positive world,

a positive love.

Oh Shame! I know where you come from.

You come from within me.

I created you.

I give you power.

I keep you alive.

Only when I begin to confront the shadows,

face the pain,

reveal the hurt —

will I be healed.

Shame, I know you.

        you are a part of me.

                By loving you I am free.

THOUGHT: God, you made me with a dignity that can never be taken away. You gave me a "greatness" that exists within; may the remembrance of this gift heal me.

NOTES

What feelings does this meditation arouse in me? _____

_____

_____

_____

_____

_____

How can I use this meditation in my life? _____

_____

_____

_____

_____

_____

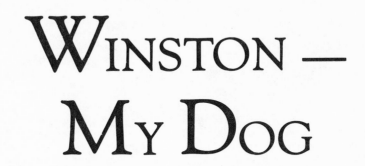

20

WINSTON — MY DOG

"If you never assumed importance, you never lost it."

Lao Tzu

"You become what you behold."

William Blake

A dog: One of God's creatures; man's best friend.

    Yes, but much more — he is my dog,

                my friend!

I've grown to love him,

    those eyes,

        that crushed-in face,

           my Winston.

He watches,

    waits,

        comforts,

           loves in perpetual silence.

                A companion and friend.

                My dog.

There was a time when I behaved like an animal to him;

                gave him a dog's life!

In those drinking days when I was lost in self.

Lonely,

    angry,

        miserable,

        confused,

           pouting on my pity-pot.

I was hurting — so I hurt others! Made sense then.

Hurt my family,

      hurt the bishop,

            kicked the dog.

                    Yes — I kicked the dog. (Not the Bishop)!

Part of my amends is to my dog.

      I can still see those large eyes staring at me.

        "Winston — please forgive me."

And I know he did.

      I know he still does — that is friendship.

Occasionally I catch him looking at me — mystified.

      Mystified, yet still accepting.

Still he watches,

      waits,

         comforts,

            loves in perpetual silence.

               A companion and friend.

              My dog.

It may seem odd but I see God in Winston.

Something in that selfless love is divine,

      in his silence I am healed,

        in his play I am revitalized,

in his face I am accepted.

My dog.

He taught me how to let go of resentments,

experience serenity,

live humility;

my dog has become my mentor.

In togetherness we live a day at a time.

GOD SAYS: The arrogance of the human animal.

I too live in MY world,

MY creation,

MY dog.

Oh, yes, Winston is also MY dog.

Man must learn from the animals;

learn how to live together and alone;

learn how to see and behold this world;

learn how to accept life in each given day.

Man thinks too small.

The animals also worshipped at the manger — in silence.

The donkey carried the King.

The cock cried at man's betrayal of himself.

Humbled divinity.

Miracle? Incarnation with a crushed face: Winston.

A THOUGHT: "What can I bring Him, poor as I am?
If I were a shepherd, I would bring a lamb."

(G.T. Holst)

Perhaps the lamb brings the shepherd?
The animal brings the man.

Lord — we still think too small.
Help us to see You in Your creatures;
Find You in Your world.

NOTES

What feelings does this meditation arouse in me? _____

_____

_____

_____

_____

How can I use this meditation in my life? _____

_____

_____

_____

_____